John W. Sexton

Inverted Night

SurVision Books

First published in 2019 by
SurVision Books
Dublin, Ireland
www.survisionmagazine.com

Copyright © John W. Sexton, 2019

Cover image © India Samhaoir Smith, 2019

Design © SurVision Books, 2019

ISBN: 978-1-912963-05-8

This book is in copyright. No part of this publication may be reproduced, stored in a retrieval system, or transmitted in any form or by any means without the prior permission in writing from the publisher.

Acknowledgements

Grateful acknowledgement is made to the editors of the following, in which these poems originally appeared:

The Irish Times, Poetry Ireland Review, Southword, SurVision, Silver Blade, Star*Line, Visions International, The Enchanting Verses, Live Encounters Poetry, A New Ulster, Pound of Flash.

And the following anthologies: *Secrets and Dreams, Switch (the Difference)*, and *Tranquillity* (all published by Kind Of A Hurricane Press and edited by A. J. Hoffman and April Salzano); *Ten Years in the Doghouse* (Doghouse Books 2013, edited by Noel King); *Five Words Anthology Volume IX 2016*, (Ó Bhéal Press, edited by Paul Casey); *The Gladstone Readings Anthology* (Famous Seamus Publishing, 2017, edited by Peter O' Neill.)

The Handbag Shaped Like a Gull & *The Cyclopean Train Approaching Kulosaari* first appeared in Street Line Critics, Helsinki, September 2015, curated by Lotte Bender.

The Dancehall on the Summit of the Bloodiest Head of the Twenty-Six-Headed Giant won The Five Words International Poetry Competition 2016.

The Snails was shortlisted in the An Post Book of the Year Awards for 2018, under the Listowel Writers' Week / An Post Irish Poem of The Year Award 2018.

CONTENTS

Earthright	5
The Snails	6
The Inverted Night	7
She Spoke Through the Letterbox	8
The Changing Room	9
The Handbag Shaped Like a Gull	10
The Seeds of Gravity	11
The Birth	12
The Poem from the Future	14
The Dancehall on the Summit of the Bloodiest Head of the Twenty-Six-Headed Giant	16
One Cognizance	17
The Weasel	18
Tin Soldier	20
Incidents of the Night	21
Wardrobe	22
The Unreturnable	23
Hedgegogs	24
Soak	26
The Woodland Beneath the Lake	28
Crown of Blood	29
The Meaning of Ceaseless, the Meaning of Infinite	30
Dancers at the Enchanted Café	31
How a Leech House Eats a House	32
Lucifer's Bulb in His Head	33
The Isn't Bus	34
Mouth to the Sky	35
The Cyclopean Train Approaching Kulosaari	36

Earthright

You, who bequeathed to us the dandelions –
an apron's worth of stars upon the meadow –
we have come to tear out your teeth as you sleep.

You cannot but sense us beside your bed.
We are that which you dream of, pulling at your mouth.
Wake now and find us gone and your mouth full of life.

You, whose mouth erupts in gobbets of scarlet flowing.
You, who will no longer bite at the heels of the morning.
You, who bequeathed to us the dandelions.

You speak the deep night that becomes our sky forever.

The Snails

The snails prove in their individual kettles.
They think you into being.
You wake for the first time but are convinced it is a numerous morning.
The newly-minted world looks the way you imagined it always was.

The garden is a square of perfect grass.
You dig it up into a square of perfect earth.
You set a perfect aspirational garden.
You sleep your first night but are convinced there were others.

You wake for the second time but think it is a numerous morning.
The glass in all of the windows is studded with snails.
You look in disgust at their oily bodies.
They threaten to become punctuations to the perfection of your hopes.

The snails are a pestilence upon your creation.
You pick them off the windows and collect them in a bucket.
You pull them from the newly-set cabbages you invented.
You created this world and will not let it be marred.

You sleep your second night.
You wake for the third time but are convinced it is a numerous morning.
On the way to somewhere there is silver writing all over the pavement.
It is a gospel you imagine always was.

The Inverted Night

She plucks a lilac star from the sky.
It becomes an anti-star scented of emptiness:

the emptiness of the heavens beyond the heavens.

One by one the stars still left in the darkness
burst into petalled flowers. The sky blooms.

She observes that this is the reality of Physics.
She presents her observations in a paper to the Academy.

The Academy look in dismay at the findings she presents.
If the universe is a poem it will be infinitely unreachable.

A man writes a number onto a whiteboard.
The number is an invention. The Academy agree

that this is the true night. On the whiteboard a universe
begins to convince us it is there.

The Academy applauds the findings on their whiteboard.
Outside, the sky drops its fragrance on one who looks up.

She Spoke Through the Letterbox

I don't have time to answer your questions
but I do have the answers. I'm running far too late
to fill in your form but if you were to wait and listen
like this a moment longer then you'd learn what I know.
The door to the snail is the snail itself,
but now it's long gone and its house
holds vacuity. Who will there ever be
to weigh the void after the snail? Is there
anyone at all who could measure the height
of its head, majestic before the beak of the thrush?
What language did you speak, Thrush, when you
snapped it out? Could anyone appreciate the quake
of the snail's buoyant body as it felt the unrelenting
power of another? Oh that snail, neither a him nor a her,
but both and neither. Well, ask me, for I have some idea.
I don't have time to open the door to let you in
but I can sense the skyline clearly from the slit.
My husband will be back soon. Although he knows nothing,
it is from him that I learnt everything. I have some idea
of the snail, helpless in its enigmatic majesty. But of course,
I'm long gone. No one had time to question my answers.

The Changing Room

In the changing room she tried on a yellow dress
and looked at herself in the long mirror.

But the yellow dress was a mask, not a dress,
so all she could see was a stranger in a blue coat.

She removed the yellow dress and tried on a blue coat.
But the blue coat was a mask, so she saw nothing

in the long mirror but the onrush of pines in her descent
from the blistered moonlit sky.

She took off the blue coat and tried on a snowy owl.
The snowy owl was a tight fit but she persevered

and squeezed herself all the way into it.
But the snowy owl was a mask, so all she could see

was herself in a yellow dress, weary from endless pretence.

The Handbag Shaped Like a Gull

Excuse me sir, but have you seen a woman
with a handbag shaped like a gull?
She would have been holding it by the tip
of its wing, and from its beak it would be
spilling the sky. If you see her enter
the underpass, do not enter after her.
Do not reach for the sky that spills
from her handbag, for it will slice
the ends off your fingers. She keeps
the sea deep in that handbag too,
and a thick sediment of money.
Be warned if you see sediment spilling
from the eye of that handbag shaped
like a gull. That is no money that you
can spend, but the blindness you get
from looking down from above.
The woman with the handbag shaped
like a gull is late for a meeting. The meeting
she is late for is the person she meets
on the way to the trains. Do not meet her.
Excuse me, my darling, but have you seen a woman
with a handbag shaped like a gull?

The Seeds of Gravity

An angel is divided into two by its wings

The right-handed wing is feathered cloud
      skies without sunset
       a slice of morning

The left-handed wing is a porcelain crescent
      embossed with glazed vines

As the angel takes flight
      the porcelain wing is shattered

Where its fragments fall
      a new wild garden is sown

With its other wing the daytime sky is born in its myriad hues

The Birth

It is dusk as the last of the cement
is flattened out in the new drive.
The clouds are dark like ripening plums
as daylight fades on the fresh mixture.
The concrete-mixer eases into the slowing traffic,
its tail-lights glistening on the dimming cement.
The clouds rupture high above.

The rain pours and pours and pours on the new cement drive.
A rhinoceros is born from the new drive in the driving rain.
The rhinoceros forces itself up,
pulling a body for itself from the thickening mix.
It stands unsteadily under the lights of the house,
four square windows of light, before taking its first step.
The rain pummels its hide but is absorbed.

The rhinoceros makes its way onto the street,
into the flow of traffic. The cars slow down.
Way ahead, with miles of a start,
is the turning womb of the concrete-mixer.
The rhinoceros plods on its way,
sniffing for the opening of its mother.

The householder steps outside his door.
His new drive is washed clean away.
The householder feels an inexplicable grief,
as if a child has just left.

In the shifting rains belonging becomes uncertain.
The householder returns inside.
All the lights go out, one by one.
Four square windows of light, one by one.

The Poem from the Future

(1) Purity of Purpose

At the Ministry of Offence the brains are fermenting in their bottles. War is being thought. On the other side of the world thousands of people fall to the ground. Thought cannot be stopped or detected. Thinking levels the Enemies of Right.

The Rhyme Sinister looks out from his window high in the Ministry of Culture. The black towers of the Ministry of Offence loom in the fog. He knows that freedom of thought must prevail. Only when thought leaves the mind is there purity of purpose. He turns from the window and faces the prisoner nailed in the kind seat. There are three other kind seats in the room but they are empty. Only the blood and faeces smeared on them suggests any past occupancy. The prisoner has his mouth sewn tight. The Rhyme Sinister thinks at him.

You have been speaking poetry. Poetry is forbidden.

The Rhyme Sinister has a poem written by the prisoner lying face-up on his desk. Going over to the desk he lifts it and reads it in his mind.

> Hellebore rips its head through the ground.
> All hellebore uprisen in its flourish. All hellebore.

What is the meaning of this? Thinks the Rhyme Sinister out loud.

The prisoner refuses to think, but instead tries to force his mouth open to form spoken words. His tongue has been rolled and pinned in place.

No sound could possibly come from his mouth. The thick thread that binds his lips is dull with blood.

The Rhyme Sinister presses a button on his desk and the kind seat containing the prisoner begins to pamper. The prisoner oozes in the kindness of the seat.

(2) Skin of the Rhyme Sinister

The Rhyme Sinister sleeps soundly in his bed. Today the last of the week's prisoners was sent to the composting pits. The latest poem to be confiscated by the Ministry of Culture has been destroyed. But poetry cannot be destroyed. It remains in the Rhyme Sinister's sleeping mind. In the Rhyme Sinister's memory the poem begins to leak through his thoughts. The Rhyme Sinister dreams of hellebore.

The poem is thought out loud and enters the room. The poem enters the carpets and the curtains and the bedding and the clothes. It enters into the skin of the Rhyme Sinister. The poem poisons everything with its innocent pervasiveness. Once the room is sated with it the poem leaves by an open window. It penetrates the air. Entering starlight it becomes manifold as direction. It travels into the future but the future is unoccuring and therefore impervious. The poem travels into the past.

The poem arrives here. Here is anywhere. Anywhere you might happen to be.

> Hellebore rips its head through the ground.
> All hellebore uprisen in its flourish. All hellebore.

The poem becomes yours. You have no idea what it means, but suddenly the present is transcendent. All hellebore.

The Dancehall on the Summit of the Bloodiest Head of the Twenty-Six-Headed Giant

The dirigible made port in the port on the side of his head.
That would be the thirteenth head. There was no option
on landing on any of his twenty-five other heads, for they
were permed and pandered for the rich and elite to frolic
in the luxury of his curls. But head number thirteen was as devoid
of hair as ever. On disembarking they were met by a stainless steel
bouncer. Pale ornamental rushes, carved from the bones of murdered
dancers, lined the fleshy streets. The bouncer struck sparks
with each step up the bone steps
                              to the dancehall on the top of the head.

The bouncer sang a song as he led the group up the steps, sang a song
through his square stainless teeth, a song of the slaughtered waltzers,
one that they had sung as they fell under the pummelling fists
of the bouncer. The bouncer's voice was deep in his steel throat,
the song was beautiful and free of pain. The other twenty-five heads
were all ears, they basked in the scandal and judged. The revel-makers
knew that this would be a dizzy weekend alright, dancing
on the bald escarpments of head number thirteen, all the other
heads talking to each other, but studiously ignoring theirs.
Yes, head number thirteen was there in the midst of all those
more superior heads, with not even its own shoulder to lean on.

One Cognizance

The sedge crowding against the husk
of a rusting motor car has no dream
in its thin many-heads. The car has
no dream either, nor memory. A beetle
skirting the edge of a puddle has the only
cognizance of dream, its pure mind
as smooth as its carapace. In an intake of breath
the beetle is crunched in the mouth of a fox.
The fox steps freely under starlight, the dream
in its mind too, the dream in its mind wide awake.
The stars seep into night, an ichor called starlight.
Starlight penetrates everything, penetrates the dark.
The dark soaks the starlight into itself, draws it in.
The dark soaks in everything, everything penetrates it.
The sedge in its thin many-headed thoughts of nothing
is imbued by every tread of beetle, fox, weasel, mouse,
swift shadows of owls; everything is touched by
and touches everything else. There is one dream,
one sleep, one cognizance wet in the ichor of starlight.

The Weasel

The weasel moves along an indiscernible path.
You may see it passing over the lawn or the meadow.

But when you go to inspect the grass
there is no residue of footfall.

The weasel pours itself forwards
in some trickery that passes for running.

The weasel steals the finch
that sings at your window.

Is there a store of finches' songs
somewhere in the weasel's den?

The weasel passes through your mind
in the form of a woman.

In that dream you had
she tied the moon with her hair.

You saw it fall slowly down the sky
until the moment you awoke.

A weasel passes over the lawn
as you look through the sunlight.

The path it moves along is as indiscernible
as when the shadows of clouds rupture the fields.

If your heart was a clock losing its time
it would be that weasel who stole it.

Tin Soldier

The tin soldier was hollow as a bell.
Which meant all the emptiness inside him
was his heart. Some, however, would discern
him heartless. My father's step crushed the shell
of him one day and all his heart leaked out.
Through my tears for my flattened trooper
all I could see was the red silk flutter
of a blood breeze. I bit my lip: my mouth
discerned the soldier's heart in everything.
Dad opened the lid of a heartless bin.
Its rancid blood poured us full of its stink.
Metal was not heartless, I realised.
But heart was whatever filled the inside.
Everything is the anything heart will ride.

Incidents of the Night

Moonlight licked grass, the still trees, the southern
windows all at once. In your sleep you turned
to the wall, breathed at its discourse of damp.
A dead moon in the corner, (shadeless lamp),
dreamt that it could dream: memories of light
in its fused mind. Outside, badgers moved night
with their sheer wills. In your sleep you turned south.
Snoring, you exhaled a cord from your mouth.
The cord shrivelled on contact with the air,
became a dribble on the pillow. Hair
gathered itself in the plughole, braided
itself; then forgot where it was headed.
From the pond a gathered-man of frogspawn,
with your name on his tongue, trod through the lawn.

Wardrobe

In a room, upon the table, is a dying fish.
The fish is gasping its last breath, but over and over,
never stopping. In that sense the fish is still alive.

A man manoeuvers his fingers into the mouth
of the fish. Carefully and deliberately he removes
a grey suit, trousers first and then the jacket.

The suit is not herringbone. Neither is it a Prince
of Wales check. The pattern on the suit is no pun
whatsoever on its residence in the fish. The suit is grey flesh.

The man dresses in the grey suit. The suit looks like death.
Carefully and deliberately the man manoeuvers his fingers
back into the mouth of the fish. He removes a tie.

The tie is the colour of a haemorrhoid. Then the man
removes a shirt. The shirt is the colour of nothing,
but the man doesn't recognise the shade. As he buttons

the collar he feels his life unravel. He knots the tie at his neck.
The man looks in a long mirror but it's smeared with light.
The man leaves the room, the fish still gasping but now alone.

The Unreturnable

In the alleyway the cats lose their shadows
to the greater shadows of the warehouses, the cats' shadows
snagged from their fur. Once out of the narrow rectum
of the alley, the cats are bright under the streetlamps,
new shadows splitting off from their bodies.
The whisper you hear therefore, crouched
in the alley as you are, is the frisson of those softly
grating shadows, thin cats of black moving through
the larger digestive tract of the alley's shadow.
This is the truth you could learn, if you stayed awake
and coherent enough: shadows consume shadows.
You sink down into the shattered fractals of crystal
meth, the moon cracking your bones as it eases itself
into the city; a cold, unconscionable tumour. Your
own shadow lost in here; unreturnable, leached of you.

Hedgegogs

Blended into invisibility by sunlight
the hedgegogs await the dusk.

In the deeps of night they sever
the cord to the moon, so that the moon turns.

Under moonlight you'll see them
if the moonlight is good and strong;
just those few nights until the cord is cut.

The hedgegogs are said to feed on the dreams of grass,
for grass dreams constantly.

The hedgegogs have spines
that reach out above the mountains,
and are often mistaken for moonlight;
the very thing the hedgegogs shy away from.

Hedgegogs are unassuming
but their company is greatly prized.

Men and women have given their entire lives
in the impossible hope of keeping one.

During the day the hedgegogs sleep
beyond the grasp
of our consciousness.

During the day we stumble about, oblivious,
carrying them everywhere;
their bodies impaled into us,
and impaling everything into everything else.

Soak

Too late does he discover
that his wardrobe is defective.
He has neglected to retain
the receipt and he is stuck with it.
The wardrobe is still green
and continues to sprout.

He opens the door and another door
is immediately at the threshold.
He opens that and another door
is behind it too. He opens door
after door to find nothing but doors.
After thirty doors he is is expecting

to get to the end of his wardrobe,
but the doors continue. Shattered
from the constant opening of doors
he falls onto his bed. The wardrobe
begins to emit birdsong but he is too
discouraged to rise. The wardrobe

displays its accordion guts
of opened doors but he can no longer
care less. What good is a wardrobe
to him that has only an opening,
but nothing beyond the opening?
Such a thing is utterly useless.

The birdsong continues to smother
the room. Too late does he realise
that the room is the receptacle
for the wardrobe's belongings.
Birdsong is in him completely.

The Woodland Beneath the Lake

The tip of the oar makes a spiral that will draw you down if you lean fingers first. Take a deep breath as you enter for the lake is all there is to breathe. Though entering fingers first you'll land on the soles of your feet. Not a single fish will you see. Sodden birds will flap past heavily but without a sound, for there's no sound down here. Beneath your feet you'll see a weak distant sun, or perhaps a moon, but it'll be always trembling. Light will rise straight up but will be swallowed in the dark silty sky. Head deep into the heart of the nearby wood and do not aim to stop. You'll stop only when you are stopped by another. Hopefully, the only one you will come upon will be an old woman sitting astride a stag, a stag covered in scales like verdigris. She will be holding a basket of buttons. Take whichever button she offers you and return at once. That button is the mind your mother lost this winter past. Only you can retrieve it; only you can return it. Do not wonder if it appears unremarkable.

Crown of Blood

The queen is murdered as she walks alone in the garden.
Her assailant is in the secret employ of her husband, the king.
An angel, invisible, is in the garden at that same moment,
deadheading ghosts from the wilted roses.

The angel pulls the heart from the dead queen's chest.
At the angel's touch the heart transforms into a scarlet crown.

As arranged, the murderer reports to the king; the king slays him.
In a cunning sleight the king sends guards to protect the queen.
The queen's ghost rises from her body.
The angel places the crown upon her spectral head.

The spirits of roses flitter about her, like scented flames.
The garden path opens downwards, slotted with steps.

The queen descends through the crust of the Earth.
At her destination she is elevated into the Earth's core.
She is now enthroned as the Queen of the Eternal Heart,
the forever beating, forever aching, forever betrayed.

The king is pleased with his deception, unaware that new borders
are being drawn, that blood is condensing in the clouds.

The Meaning of Ceaseless, the Meaning of Infinite

Somewhere outside, indeterminate,
(a verge of roadside), thistles are scraping
the night. Parts of the darkness are flaking,
drifting with the wind. Insensate,

the seeds of night blossom into more night.
This is all there is then: endless corrosion
of night into night, the fading vision,
the mind lost, thoughts trapped like pomegranate

gems jellied into both sweet and bitter;
one taste promising another better,
but each presenting its endless other.

And in the morning? Just thistles eroding
the air; until the sky shifts on its hinge,
as night and day present their endless other.

Dancers at the Enchanted Café

After the painting "The Enchanted Café" by Rex Sexton

Cakes made of starlight
rise by the open window.
A comet scatters its trail
of ancient futures.

The husband's suit
is made of weeping:
a clear blue
of splendid tears.

From his bracelet of gold
dangle the stars.
He is joined by the wrist
to the sky.

His wedding ring
is a braid of his partner's hair;
she dances with blood
in her glass.

A gypsy's ghost
with a violin
keeps them nimbly
stepping.

How a Leech House Eats a House

The builders moved in on the twenty-third,
arrived with no notice of their coming.
In the long months they were seen but not heard,
for dead hammering is no hammering.
Rooms appeared inside our own; bright, spectral
as frogspawn jelly; eyeless, yes, but cold.
Superimposed, rooms shone electrical
when the lights were off; our windows blazed bold
lozenges through night. New tenants settled
into us, our bones lit from within. Time
lost its meaning, space became unsettled
until we were simply shadows, a mime
cast by the new dwellers. Our tenancy
done, we entered eternal vacancy.

Lucifer's Bulb in His Head

Brains to burn, his mind was a lump of lard.
When he thought, he thought his thoughts unheard;
strains of binary pathways, strings of code.
Hens pecked at the thinking he'd left scattered.
Archetypes were scratched in the mud by claws
of angels fallen to the mucky yard;
though not the Angels of God – but simply
parasites moving through Heaven. Nine, nine,

nine, nine: sigils stark with emergency.
Listen, listen. Hold vigils for the voice
of reason. Not the voice of yourself, not
thoughts birthing grey mould like his thoughts birthed.
Brains to burn, his mind was a lump of lard;
when he thought, his thoughts were deathly loud.

The Isn't Bus

An eye has risen over the city
and weeps its green lye. The city is as thin
as light; it blinks in and out; here now, gone now.
The street is and isn't. I take the isn't bus.
At the lights the bus is. On entering the bus station
the bus isn't. We disembark into a pale flame.
Moths as large as coats expire as smoke
in the air around us. A woman begins combing
sound from her hair. The sound flocks
in the brightness above us, a liquid ball of dark;
it coagulates over the city. One by one
single chimes fall from the sky. The concrete forecourt
of the bus station is littered with starlings,
now fluttering soundlessly at our feet.
A man removes faces from his briefcase
and distributes them to everyone nearby.
The face he has given me is disconsolate. I pull it over
my head and it slips into place. Another bus
enters the station and we embark. We ask
to be taken nowhere and the driver kills the
engine. In the stillness of the darkened bus
we wait without any expectation whatsoever.

Mouth to the Sky

The speckled thrush stepped onto the sunlight conveyer-belt to the hedge-depth and was gone into shadow. Somewhere in there the thrush became a cat, or was eaten by a cat, or killed the cat and wore it as a coat; but out the far perimeter of the hedge emerged the cat. The cat approached the opened door of the car, the car shining black like a soul, a soul of darkness so pure that the sun turned it white as a flash. Out the other side of the car stepped a woman in a black coat, a coat so black it absorbed the sun. She opened her mouth to the sky and out came the song of the speckled thrush.

The Cyclopean Train Approaching Kulosaari

The man with the umbrella made from bats' wings
is shaking the rain into your face. Each raindrop
is the memory of a missed train. In each train
is a woman with freckles like the spots on a lynx.
Then her face is a lynx's face; there's a pleading
songbird between her teeth. The umbrella
of bats' wings takes to the air, makes a path
through the clouds of flies that have been deputised
as the sun. Suddenly the sun is shattered
into fragments of black glass. You pick a piece
from the ground and your finger bleeds straight away.
It bleeds uncontrollably and you have no choice
but to put your finger into your mouth. Then a train as red
as your bloody finger enters the platform. It is the train
that you have missed all your life. The doors open
with a hiss. The sky above is a deep green. Now is now.

More poetry published by SurVision Books

Noelle Kocot. *Humanity*
(New Poetics: USA)
ISBN 978-1-9995903-0-7

Ciaran O'Driscoll. *The Speaking Trees*
(New Poetics: Ireland)
ISBN 978-1-9995903-1-4

Helen Ivory. *Maps of the Abandoned City*
(New Poetics: England)
ISBN 978-1-912963-04-1

Elin O'Hara Slavick. *Cameramouth*
(New Poetics: USA)
ISBN 978-1-9995903-4-5

Anatoly Kudryavitsky. *Stowaway*
(New Poetics: Ireland)
ISBN 978-1-9995903-2-1

George Kalamaras. *That Moment of Wept*
ISBN 978-1-9995903-7-6

Anton Yakovlev. *Chronos Dines Alone*
(Winner of James Tate Poetry Prize 2018)
ISBN 978-1-912963-01-0

Bob Lucky. *Conversation Starters in the Language No One Speaks*
(Winner of James Tate Poetry Prize 2018)
ISBN 978-1-912963-00-3

Christopher Prewitt. *Paradise Hammer*
(Winner of James Tate Poetry Prize 2018)
ISBN 978-1-9995903-9-0

Mikko Harvey & Jake Bauer. *Idaho Falls*
(Winner of James Tate Poetry Prize 2018)
ISBN 978-1-912963-02-7

Maria Grazia Calandrone. *Fossils*
Translated from Italian
(New Poetics: Italy)
ISBN 978-1-9995903-6-9

Sergey Biryukov. *Transformations*
Translated from Russian
(New Poetics: Russia)
ISBN 978-1-9995903-5-2

Anton G. Leitner. *Selected Poems 1981–2015*
Translated from German
ISBN 978-1-9995903-8-3

Our books are available to order via
http://survisionmagazine.com/books.htm

www.ingramcontent.com/pod-product-compliance
Lightning Source LLC
Chambersburg PA
CBHW061312040426
42444CB00010B/2609